The Permeation of Tears

Andrew Beattie

Index

Introduction 3
My Yesterday 4
Unforgiving clay 6
Tears of despair 7
Down memory lane 8
For a moment 9
The bitter fuelled night 10
The morgue yawns 11
Trouble 12
Struggling 13
The Nothing Effect 14
A Belfast love letter 15
Freedom Shore 16
Bare of Reason 17
The Ageing of time 18
Garden of Eden 19
No empathy 21
Philistine 22
Past thoughts 23
A child's perspective 24
Fragments of deprivation 25
A safety haven 26
Victims 27
Full moon 28
Abbeydale 29
Only you 30
Ancient Insecurities 31
Monastic pain 32
Tribulation festers 33
I remember back 34
A sympathetic notion 35

Introduction

I was born in 1964 which made me five years of age when the troubles in Northern Ireland first broke out.

I grew up in the protestant side of Ardoyne and witnessed some of the worst violence in North Belfast. From the early 1970's and right through the 1980's.

The people sadly accepted this as normality, Going about their daily business, living and surviving as best they could.

It was very sad to see the two communities rip each other apart through the use of terrorist organisations, who maimed and killed just because a person came from the other side of the religious divide.

These are my poems which are based around these cruel times. I hope you the reader can get some sort of insight into these events. And by reading my poetry I hope you can reflect for a few moments and feel the sheer madness we had to endure.

My Yesterday

Looking through the windows of my bruised soul I can see the Glenbryn of my yesterday
Where children played innocently until nightfall in broken glass strewn streets
Paramilitary murals always played a major part in the ghetto I called my home
The air was normally filled with bullets, petrol bombs and civil unrest

Just outside my house sat two rather large iron drums, one at either side of the road
Another two sat in the very same manner at the bottom of my street
All the streets in the neighbourhood were manufactured and fashioned in the same way
The inside of the drums were crudely caked with cement holding in place weighty metal poles, which spread across each road
This was our defence mechanism from terrorists who desperately wanted to enter our streets to cause havoc and mayhem

Sadly that was accepted as normality growing up in the early nineteen seventies in working class areas of Belfast
I can hardly say I miss those terrifying old days which the locals simply call 'The Troubles'
So many agonising and pitiful tears falling from crushed hearts languishing on both sides of the divide
I utterly despised the cruelty as a confused young boy
Every time a car drove slowly past me I always thought maybe I'm going to be the latest victim
As in the city centre when bombs blew limbs off the innocent, with their blood flowing cheaply into the very gutter

Yes life was regarded as nothing back then, it could be taken from you merely for being in the wrong place at the wrong time
Simply coming from the other side of the divided corrugated iron barrier
When orange shot green and vice versa it was unjustified and morally wrong
The evil of this province had risen its ugly head repeatedly
And supplied us generously with bigotry and destruction with death the ultimate victor

The scales of burning hatred blinding their demonic possessed eyes
Filled fiery red, battle scarred and full of revengeful rage, I don't miss the eerie deadly silence of my yesterday
When persistent pessimism and negativity dominated the Ulster sky

Thank God! This new optimistic generation has not been inflicted with a grief stricken element

We can never genuinely forget our yesterday for many are physically or mentally scarred for the rest of their lives

But let us strive, hope and pray for a peaceful and prosperous future for all our children and our children's children

Unforgiving clay

They nailed the board above your face
Such a waste, my heart did race
Very soon amongst unforgiving clay
No more to see the break of day

Nothing much exists for long in this life
Except for trouble with all its strife
Then to be impatiently cast aside
From this world let me now hide

Raised above an ungodly mound
Nothing picturesque, no spring-like sound
Though the rain has finally fled
Only emptiness fills a silenced head

This Northern Irish landscape what have you done to me
Will you ever set me free?
I have wanted to run to foreign land
So many times my head lay buried in quicksand

The wind is now light
The nights are long and bright
Sun and moon dance with glowing joy
Though I feel disconnected like a little lost boy

Being poor I had only my dreams
Tainted by reality and half-hearted schemes
At last at ease under unforgiving clay
Taking the natural simplistic way

Tears of despair

I believe in God
Though not man's deception
Who fires up deep division
Through blind bigotry

I watched so-called ethnic cleansing
As a bewildered small boy
Friends had to leave my street
The naked eye does not see mental scars

Burning buses and smashed up homes
A city divided through hatred
Misguided by angry voices
Blood shed on a violent path

Tears of despair fill a Belfast sky
Shots ring out night after night
Bomb after bomb destroying our land
Where had sanity gone in a time of need

Reliable boxes lie side by side
Under the crust of Ulster's soil
No more suspicion, no more
Just the eerie silence of nothing

Down memory lane

Disorientation engulfs my tragic environment
How cruel this depraved world can be
Even through refreshing summer rays
Desperate depression takes hold

Niggling criticism devours every living cell
Violating my very bone marrow
Calamity and disarray
Leave a heavy price
Down memory lane, falling
Forcing myself up, falling yet again

For a moment

Doors open filling my mind
For a moment I thought you were alive
Unsmiling shrugs of discontent
The stuttering of words

The dream tasted heavenly, master of disguise
Reality challenges my very existence
The garden now in full bloom
Pity you're not here to share

Birds singing their hearts are content
Dreamy blue skies rejoice
Fluffy Milky clouds float tenderly by
For a moment, I thought

The bitter fuelled night

He was my best friend, wee Joe
Who had a sister called Barbara
Their parents were called Joe and Barbara as well

My parents were having a late night out
And Mum Barbara said I could stay with them
An ordinary decent family
Just going about their normal daily duties

I awoke in the early hours
To the sound of bullets ripping through the house
I was frightened to pieces
Shaking and deeply disturbed
I still decided to get up
As more bullets ripped through the house

Mum Barbara called me into their room – with concern and worry
She held me in her bosom like one of her own
Shielding and protecting me from stray bullets
As young Barbara and Joe lay in their father's arms

Tears flowed down my cheeks out of despair
Was I to die from these vile metal cases
It seemed like a warzone from a John Wayne film
Only this was for real

We survived the bitter fuelled night
As the security forces eventually arrived on the scene
But my mind would never be the same again
Forever haunted by visions from our wicked past

The morgue yawns

Dusted with frost
Bitten by the past
Aching memories fester
Granite shoulders struggle

Painting a picture in my mind
Reflective – through a heavy heart
Day after day
Imperfection – train of thought

Much hardship
Striking in its prime
Whispering smoothly to the innocent
Flatter – with a merry dance

The morgue yawns
Shadow – close
Inability to cope
Withdrawn

Trouble

Trouble will find you, it will come your way
Occupying gravely thoughts without delay
Holding you in captivity it will enslave
Taking hold to a mysterious grave

You can only keep it at bay for so long
It toys with the soul, so wrong
Bringing confusion and destruction under hypnotic spell
Languishing in the depths of hell

Casting a hideous eye
Heart-rending you want to die
Leaving my comfortable safe bubble
Oh that criminal word, trouble!

Struggling

Everything turns to black when struggling
Mind wants to grasp tranquillity but can't
High winds play havoc with weary body
Strong currents summon from below ferocious waves

Lost child wandering through dense forest
Silence deadly silence lingers in the atmosphere
Trees shake violently as they seemingly try to grab
Have to leave this bizarre place

I try, I really do
Oh but I can't seem to get very far
The stench of rotten human flesh makes me vomit severely
Can you not see that I am truly struggling…

The Nothing Effect

I need an attempt at reality to help me find clarity
The winter weeks pass so slowly
Not one soul comes knocking upon my door
No long lost friend, not one glimmer of hope

Curtains wave from the January draft
Which attacks my fragile chest through weakened single glazed windows
The streets in my city lie tarnished and crippled from the past
Leaving lonely bruised people in its wake

My mind dwells on morbid self-pity
Racing over so many deep memories
I miss someone to hold on these shambolic nights
Lost, afraid and all alone

The wind teases and pokes fun
As empty tin cans rattle along the street
A plastic bag hangs manically in the air
Without due care over its destination

Bored senseless my mind goes blank
In a perverse way I like the nothing effect
It brings the emptiness to a fulfilling head
Perhaps I am plain and simply dead

A Belfast love letter

Peering into still water
I see a true force of nature
Like delicate pollen on my shoulder
The wakening of artistic mind

Beautiful, tangible optimism
Swims in the River Lagan
Through murky, putrid water
For hope shines in the darkest of places

Rough local voices captivate me
Actively engaging in conversation
Bags of gossip enjoying solidarity
Small talk lingers around Belfast streets

Catholic Falls and Protestant Shankill
Share common ground
Under the surface they find a kindred spirit
Each suffering from life's agonies

Belfast is where I grew up
The city that I love
From the atrocious days of the past
To building a positive future for all its people

Freedom Shore

The echo of love revisited
Fortunate that memories still flourish
Disturbing the cradle of genius
Which stands the passing of time

Indifference through sedation
Pales into insignificance
Suffering an influx of criticism
A heavy price for individuality

You plagiarize my every thought
Natural spring to cure my complexities
Finding no favour
Flames continue to rise
Igniting a forest fire

Water lapping by freedom shore
I seek refuge not hostility
Throwing myself to the elements, defying logic
A cry, a cry for redemption

Bare of Reason

Life is but a shadow
Which disappears into the night
Falling from grace
Through bitterest pill

It demands respect
Though we don't always give
For in our youth we reject
All its advice with agile arrogance

Biting when we least expect
Having the last laugh
Casting gut to the four corners
Bare of reason

The permeation of tears
Binds with gravely bones
To a place we go, not humane
Driving the mind mentally insane

The Ageing of time

I walk along Mullaghmore Harbour
And meet the ghostly fragments of Mountbatten
Hands held out looking for sympathy
Weeping amongst stagnant water which tantalises pathetic remains

The sprawling estate still pours down from the hill
To lord it over such common folk
Far removed from the rest of civilisation
Nothing has changed, no nothing

With postcard picturesque beauty
Who could have imagined this happening here
What an embarrassment in seventy-nine
The people were in a daze
Sure they're laid back Irish they'll be fine

Seagulls squawk in the Sligo air
Fluffy clouds float idly past a pale blue sky
Part of me wants to leap into the water to refresh my mood
Fragmented not by bomb but by the ageing of time

I sit with my milky Guinness in hand and dream of tomorrow
The majestic Ben Bulben stands proudly in the distance
I seek a genius in Drumcliff below
Whose mortal voice has long since gone
His steely words of wisdom have not

Though the world weeps with many a sorrow
I'll smile and rest beside a simple grave
And quote my timeless friend
For the creativity of literature has no end

Garden of Eden

Mist eerily creeps over the Belfast Hills
Accompanied by haunting rain
The night looks moody and menacing
Darkness ready to play havoc

It is the first day of June
Something lurks in the shadow
I toy with mystical illusion
For life is but a game of chance

Part of me wants to keep walking forever
Part of me wants to hide from reality
Another part simply wants to die
None of which is particularly clever

Spring and Summer are cruellest of all
Those bright adorable nights
You are not here to share
For now you live under the earth's crust

The alcohol is wearing off
It leaves me deeply scarred
With long and dark lonely thoughts
Added with desperate depression

Tears quickly fall onto a worthless world
Creating a pool of sorrow
The mind is plagued by confusion
For I cannot hold you in my arms anymore

I lie with grief on the bedroom floor
The heart is crushed into tiny particles
Nothing seems to matter now
Except endless thoughts of you

I see a ghost happily grinning
Dancing freely in a garden of Eden
You make a daisy chain and attach it to my wrist
Then blow me a tender kiss

Sunshine smiles upon your shoulder
Mesmerizing sky luminous for the world to see
I watch your spirit ascend into the stratosphere

As the gates of heaven wait with anticipation

No empathy

Banks of fog dupe my senses
Swamped with isolation and fear
I cannot focus a clear path
Tears flow easily from concern

Gunfire plagues my weary and battered land
Along with the mighty roar of bombs exploding
Wave after wave of torment
Leaves broken dreams washed up on a shore

Deserts of hurt collide
They show no empathy
Hope fades with falling winter light
Morals detached through bitter hatred

The wind of conception carries
Until the echo of disturbance subsides
I let the air of mysticism take me
While ghostly figures loom

Philistine

You are nothing but a philistine who leads the majority down an insecure and dangerous path
Brutalising and terrorising the whole community with fascist actions and remarks
A bully who encourages division, hatred and violence
Embarrassingly pathetic whilst barking out orders to a lost and blinded tribe
The leader of a pack of wolves ready to devour the organic traces of natural living organism

Art and culture indisputably miles away from your intolerant, submerged and barren head
Boastfully bragging, small minded and uncouth inside a demoralised wasteland
Uncontrollable and despising anything which has a shred of human decency or dignity
Arrogantly conceited while flexing your military muscle ruthlessly

Bitterness sweeps down easily from your hardened heart
A danger to every rightful thinking person on this part of the island
Cruelly replenishing and hatefully sowing the seed of evil ways
Loathing the philistine with utter contempt
With his twisted scheming and uncultured kind

Past thoughts

Standing at the door
Ancient wood calling
Wind howls to a new level
Echoes burn deep within

Dancing trees keep an eagle eye
Birds squawk desperately throughout volatile air
Heavy water falls from disheartening sky
Mother of storms approaching

Mind playing devious games
Curtains gloomy and mischievous
Groans of weariness lie just beyond
Past thoughts scatter to far off places

Mountainous splendour captures with anticipation
Lips chapped by the elements
Frost permeates a brittle chest
Eyes wide and wretched with fear

A child's perspective

Stranded at Carlisle Circus
Looking to Dad to cool my fear
The absence of words
Leaves fractured resilience

From the dock only an hour before
Faces strewn in torment
Bomb after bomb explodes in my city
We seek refuge behind the Statue of Reverend Roaring Hanna

Carnage at Oxford Street Bus Station
Pieces of burning flesh concealed
Like meat carved for gratification
Barbarism in highest form

Bloody Friday was meant to be a glorious homecoming
Belfast the City that I love
Blinded by hatred
Fragmented by gelignite

I'm only an innocent child
No blood on my hands
Suffer little children and forbid them not to come onto me
For of such is the kingdom of heaven

Fragments of deprivation

Fragments of deprivation come flooding
Surging into the eye of the ferocious storm
Battle scarred from a cruel element
A twist of fate falls on my impoverished body
Angry skies threaten to pound my brittle head
Belfast streets can come across mean and suspicious to the outsider
Devaluing many a poor working class boy
Who has often been put through a barbaric mangle
Demoralised by the tragedies of life

A safety haven

Walking aimlessly over Divis and Black Mountain
Peering down below onto a war-torn fragile city
Embracing the rough terrain for it suits my solemn mood
Panting and out of breath as I reach the blustery summit

My boots are covered in the muddiest of soil
With pale skin freezing from harsh elements
I don't really care at this poignant moment in time
Wanting to hide below raw stones which engulfs your pleasant landscape
A safety haven which is pleasing to the honourable eye

You promised that you would light a candle for me
Praying endlessly and fervently for my soul to be redeemed
You always were a devoted follower of the banner of truth
Right now in my life I need divine inspiration
A heavenly mystical miracle

Victims

Why am I still on the outside
I should be languishing within
Weary and drugged souls wander pathetically around
Will they ever actually be free
Lost backgrounds with impoverished darkened futures
Why does society toy with their very existence
Sobering, harrowing and contemplating thoughts indeed

Shadows lurk eerily for evermore
Slow dragging footsteps scrape along the ground
While the frightening sound of chains clanking, closer by the moment
Now they seem only a hair's breath away

Full moon

Looking from my back bedroom window
I see the full moon protruding in the melancholy sky
Pale orange with dark grey clouds drifting past its face
Wishing I could reach out and touch it
Even for just a moment in the miraculous spellbound air

I wonder what its thinking
Pity it couldn't tell you what lies beyond
So many of life's historic magical and tragic events it has witnessed since time began
This mass of energy peers down upon our every moment
Standing proud like a majestic beacon through the wary witching hours

If only it could speak its true mind to the world
What it thinks and what it feels when analysing from above
Can anyone get a real sense or true purpose of its divine wisdom
Perhaps protecting mankind like a demigod
For we struggle with uncertainty in this mortal life

We argue, fight and persist with stubbornness in our natural daily existence
Made of fragile bones, flesh and blood
With a harbour of distasteful weakness
Though the full moon lingers in the dead of night bringing some hope
With a magnetic force mesmerising from a heavenly place

Abbeydale

Walking round the peaceful, tranquil and satisfying Abbeydale
A beautiful hidden pocket in north Belfast
It has a taste of bewildering freshness which spouts glorious sunshine
Bountiful to me in so many poetical ways

Through the spine-tingling dead of night I yearn for you
Kept away from religious bigotry – which eats away at many a cold heart
Spreading rapidly like a blistering forest fire
Cover me with your affectionate and timeless inspiration

Proud elegant houses stand in defiance against the nastiness languishing in the north Belfast air
Straight smart streets inviting and welcoming with open arms
Walking around in a dream like state
Abbeydale you provoke and probe me to a higher plane

Only you

I carry the weight of the world with just two hands
The tears fall with grace
Sensitive to a desperate world
Which aches from so many agonies

I am sad for the way things are right now
Warped minds play with innocent blood
Take a moment out from life and just ponder over the skies
For they light up like flames straight out of hell

Pray fervently from your very soul
For our fight is not with flesh and blood
Not of sheer military might
It is a spiritual battle ringing from heaven

Come and take my honest hand
Let us bow our heads with sincerity
To a God that will never forsake
The world cries out and anxiously awaits
For only you can quench a lifeless thirst

Ancient Insecurities

Always walking a lonely path frightened and terribly alone
Belfast streets cry out with the sound of wailing sirens
Death and destruction sweeps over pleasant green land
No more can we bury our head in faceless sand

Creeping through narrow streets and side door entrances
With weary legs and worn out shoes
False smiles approach left feeling awkward
Ancient insecurities slumber in tribal ancestral tradition

Life is like the early morning mist
Here for a little while then it's completely gone
Anguished tears scream from four decaying walls
The faithful sound of bullets whistle past your head

Within a minute I could be silenced forever
Lying slain on blood stained tarnished ground
No more worldly passions entering my silenced head
Train of thought awkwardly exposed and unforgivably dead

Monastic pain

I drink to forget that I'm talking to a repetitive machine
Tonight I hide in a mound of myth
Far beyond anything known to mankind
In the morning I'm too hungover to remember the sterile boredom

Transfixed with a delicate thought
Too selfish to contemplate tedious reflection
Ah thank God for the whiskey bottle
And thank God for genius though it pains

Utter contempt for the tribal concrete jungle
That plunges me into deep despair
I read an obituary of simple daily life
Where nothing but ugliness follows a weary path

The rain pours down day after day
Relentless just like dreary mouths
Small talk, all small talk
Where are the devilish inquisitive minds?

One door closes then another and another
Monastic pain is not simply mind over matter
It's something I have to crawl into
A way of life to cleanse and purify the soul
Far away from the echo of vulgar voices
And heartless minds

Tribulation festers

Trudging over those desolated streets
Biting the hand that feeds
Reflecting through a heavy heart
Tribulation festers in utter confusion

Plastic vendetta smiles come forth
Pulling punches for the sake of sanity
Left to groan in glass strewn path
Forgotten by a world that does not care

I remember back

They were our next door neighbours
Decent, respectable and Roman Catholic
They would have done anything for you
As the old saying goes

Every Friday when Miriam and Pauline came home from work
My friend Michael and I surrounded them for pocket money
Please Auntie Miriam, please Auntie Pauline we both would say at the same time
They were always more than willing to share

Their sister Betty was my sister's best friend
A brother called Aidan had died in a motorbike accident aged seventeen, how tragic
The parents were quiet and hard working
Other offspring were much older and I cannot recollect their names or nature

I remember back to that night with total sadness
And the people who carried out these cruel deeds with disdain
The angry voices who woke me up with pure hatred in their very veins
"No not that house it's next door
That's where the fenians live"
As they taunted and jeered

I heard the violent sound of a window smashing into pieces
Then another and another one
Again and again and again
Until every window was smashed to smithereens

The family lay sprawled helpless on the bathroom floor
As they tried in vain to seek shelter and some comfort
My parents could do nothing for they were terrified of repercussions
An eerie silence lingered in the witching hour and beyond
Nazi style ethnic cleansing with all its sickening glorification

Next morning the Trainors said their final goodbyes
With tears trickling down their cheeks and ours
How sad to see lovely people leaving the street for the last time
To this day I have never had neighbours so unassuming as the Trainors

A sympathetic notion

Many times we carry much weight on burdened shoulders
In wanting to put the world to right
We need to hold the cup of human decency firmly
And with sincerity
For life is so short

To reach out to the other side
Go with clarity bearing no ill will
Empathetic thoughts need to be addressed
Through the eye of realism
Through the heart of idealism

Printed in Poland
by Amazon Fulfillment
Poland Sp. z o.o., Wrocław